MEGAWORDS 3
Multisyllabic Words for Reading, Spelling, and Vocabulary

KRISTIN JOHNSON   **POLLY BAYRD**

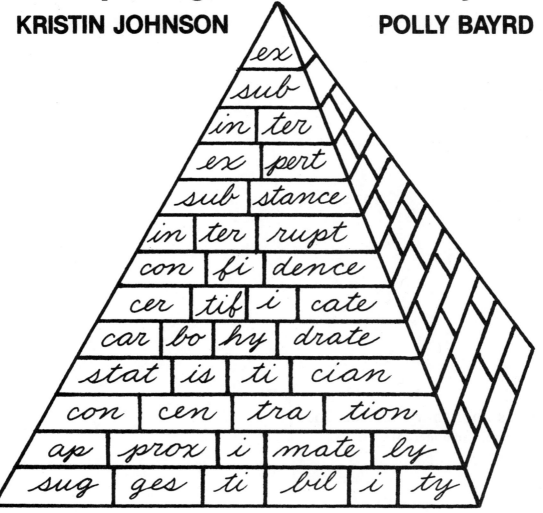

Educators Publishing Service, Inc.
Cambridge and Toronto

Educators Publishing Service, Inc.
31 Smith Place, Cambridge, MA 02138

Contents

To the Student iv

List 15: /əl/ and /ĭk/ Endings 1

List 16: /ĭt/ and /ət/ Endings 12

List 17: Middle-Syllable Schwa 28

List 18: /ənt/ and /əns/ Endings 38

List 19: Unaccented Endings *-ive*, *-ice*, *-ace*, *-ine*, and *-ain* 51

Review: Lists 15-19 66

Summary of Accent Patterns 68

Accuracy Checklist 70

Proficiency Graph 71

Examiner's Recording Form 75

TO THE STUDENT

Megawords 3: Multisyllabic Words for Reading, Spelling, and Vocabulary is the third in a series of books designed to help you read and spell words that contain two or more syllables. The words are organized into lists according to their phonetic structure. Worksheets following each list explain and help you practice the rules or patterns found in that particular group of words. Some exercises focus on reading the words; others focus on spelling or vocabulary.

Megawords is designed to meet your individual learning needs. You and your teacher can decide which lists you need to study (and which you already know) by interpreting your results on the Check Test. You may need to focus on reading *and* spelling. Or you may need to use *Megawords* only to improve spelling skills. You and your teacher can record your progress on the Accuracy Checklist at the back of your book.

We think that it is important for you to be able to 1) sound out words and 2) learn to read them proficiently and fluently. You and your teacher will set a reading rate goal. When you can read the words easily and automatically, you will be less likely to forget the words and you can concentrate on reading for meaning instead of on sounding out words. You can keep track of your reading rate on the Proficiency Graph at the end of your book.

Megawords 3 focuses on unaccented ending patterns and unaccented middle syllables with a schwa or short-*i* vowel sound. These words can be hard to spell. *Megawords 3* shows you patterns and gives you the skills to make spelling these words easier. *Megawords 3* also shows you how to use accent patterns to help sound out multisyllabic words.

We hope that you will be interested in checking out your skills in reading and spelling multisyllabic words—in seeing what you know and what you need to learn. In addition, we hope that you will enjoy tackling new word groups and mastering them. We think that multisyllabic words, when presented clearly and in patterned groups, can be challenging and fun. We sincerely hope that you enjoy and experience success with *Megawords*.

Polly Bayrd
Kristin Johnson

LIST 15: /əl/ AND /ĭk/ ENDINGS

-al=/əl/	-al=/əl/	-ic=/ĭk/	-ic=/ĭk/
*final	*hospital	*picnic	artistic
oral	*arrival	*comic	*athletic
vocal	*general	*logic	sarcastic
mental	*several	*music	*electric
formal	*personal	*plastic	*Pacific
*dental	liberal	panic	allergic
tidal	*mineral	static	arsenic
pedal	reversal	frantic	atomic
*normal	interval	*clinic	ceramic
*real	*national	garlic	*terrific
*local	optional	critic	prolific
mortal	decimal	arctic	*fantastic
global	*natural	mystic	*gigantic
coastal	eternal	skeptic	energetic
*loyal	*capital	*public	*democratic
*legal	external	*traffic	patriotic
*central	*federal	*basic	*geographic
*metal	*funeral	*Atlantic	catastrophic
royal	criminal	heroic	academic
vital	*actual	angelic	acrobatic
*trial	accidental	anemic	systematic
plural	terminal	statistic	*automatic
dismal	admiral	phonetic	characteristic
fiscal	cardinal	*elastic	
*signal	*animal		
coral	removal		
spinal			

*Practical spelling words. The teacher and student should decide together how many of these words the student will be responsible for spelling.

1

The schwa (ə) sounds like short *u*. The schwa sound is always found in unaccented syllables. *-al* is an unaccented ending with a schwa sound. *-al* says /əl/.

Pronounce and combine the syllables. Then cover the divided word and practice reading the whole word. Circle the *-al* ending as shown.

fi	nal		fin**al**
vo	cal		vocal
for	mal		formal
ped	al		pedal
ti	dal		tidal
in	ter	val	interval

e	ter	nal	eternal
lib	er	al	liberal
sev	er	al	several
ar	ri	val	arrival
min	er	al	mineral
per	son	al	personal

Match the syllables to make a real word. Then say the word as you write it. Make two words in each group.

den		sig		plas	
lo	tal	stat	nal	lo	cal
hos	pi	ex	ter	vo	

_____   _____   _____

_____   _____   _____

dec	i	loy			plur		
gar	mal	fan	tas	al	gen	er	al
nor		re			com		

_____   _____   _____

_____   _____   _____

Unscramble these three-syllable words.

mal i an _____   tal cap i _____

2

WORKSHEET 15-B

-ic is an unaccented ending that says /ĭk/

Pronounce and combine the syllables. Then cover the divided word and practice reading the whole word. Circle the *-ic* ending as shown.

pic	nic			picn(ic)
fran	tic			frantic
clin	ic			clinic
gar	lic			garlic
e	las	tic		elastic
ar	sen	ic		arsenic

fan	tas	tic		fantastic
ter	rif	ic		terrific
e	lec	tric		electric
sys	tem	at	ic	systematic
At	lan	tic		Atlantic
sar	cas	tic		sarcastic

Match the syllables to make a real word. Then say the word as you write it. Make two words in each group.

plas			gi	gan		pho	net	
loy	tic		na	tion	tic	pan		ic
fran			At	lan		ped		

_____   _____   _____

_____   _____   _____

coast			a	tom		ac	ro	bat	
clin	ic		plur		ic	e	ter		ic
crit			com			en	er	get	

_____   _____   _____

_____   _____   _____

Unscramble these three-syllable words.

let ath ic _____   tic tis ar _____

cif ic Pa _____   ro he ic _____

3

WORKSHEET 15-C

Your teacher will dictate some words. Sound them out as you write the missing letters. Then write the whole word, saying it aloud as you spell it.

	Copy	ABC Order
1. _ _ _ ic	_____	_____
2. _ _ _ _al	_____	_____
3. _ _ _ _ _ic	_____	_____
4. _ _ _ _al	_____	_____
5. _ _ _ _ic	_____	_____
6. _ _ _ _ _ al	_____	_____
7. _ _ _ _ _ _ _ _ ic	_____	_____
8. _ _ _ _ _ _al	_____	_____
9. _ _ _ _ _ _al	_____	_____
10. _ _ _ _ _ _ _ic	_____	_____

Now go back and write the words in alphabetical order.

Decide whether the following words end with *al* or *ic*. Add the ending that makes a real word, and then copy the whole word.

gi gan t_ _ _____   gen er _ _ _____

in ter v_ _ _____   per son _ _ _____

min er _ _ _____   au to mat _ _ _____

ar ri v_ _ _____   ac ro bat _ _ _____

ar tis t_ _ _____   ge o graph _ _ _____

crim in _ _ _____   car di n_ _ _____

e lec tr_ _ _____   ac ci den t_ _ _____

Review: The schwa sounds like short _____. The schwa sound is always found in

_____ syllables.

-al is an unaccented ending that has the _____ sound.

4

-al is an unaccented ending that says /əl/. The accent is on another syllable in the word.

In two- and three-syllable words, accent the first syllable. Then pronounce the first vowel as if it were a short, long, *r*-controlled, or double-vowel sound in a one-syllable word (*fi′ nal, min′ er al*).[1] If that doesn't make a recognizable word, accent the second syllable, and pronounce the second vowel according to its syllabic type.

The dark lines and accent marks in this book are *accent patterns* (__′ __). Each line stands for one syllable. The accent mark shows you which syllable is accented.

Draw a box around the accented syllable, and then copy the word by syllables.

Two-Syllable Words __′ __

*legal   *le gal*

*central __ __ __   __ __ __

formal __ __ __   __ __ __

vital __ __   __ __ __

*local __ __   __ __ __

*trial __ __ __   __ __ __

Three-Syllable Words __′ __ __

*several __ __ __   __ __ __

*personal __ __ __   __ __ __

optional __ __   __ __ __ __

*hospital __ __ __   __ __   __ __ __

*funeral __ __   __ __ __   __ __

*federal __ __ __   __ __ __

Sometimes you accent the second syllable in three-syllable words (__ __′ __).

Draw a box around the accented syllable, and then copy the word by syllables.

eternal __   __ __ __   __ __ __

reversal __ __   __ __ __   __ __ __

*arrival __ __   __ __ __   __ __ __

external __ __   __ __ __   __ __ __

removal __ __   __ __ __   __ __ __

Have another student test you on spelling the starred words. They are practical spelling words.

My score: _____ words correct.

[1]A Summary of Accent Patterns is on pages 68 and 69.

WORKSHEET 15-E

-ic is an unaccented ending that says /ĭk/. The accent is on the syllable just before the ending *-ic*.

In the following words, find the accented syllable, and then copy the words by syllables under the correct heading. Write the accented syllables in the boxes.

garlic	democratic	comic
fantastic	Arctic	artistic
geographic	sarcastic	academic
music	systematic	characteristic
elastic	gigantic	

Accent the First Syllable

gar *lic*

Accent the Second Syllable

Accent the Third Syllable

Accent the Fourth Syllable: _____ _____ _____ ☐ _____

6

Adding the ending -al to a word sometimes changes the accent pattern. The stress may move to a different syllable when you add -al.

de part' ment ⟶ de part men' tal

ac' ci dent ⟶ ac ci den' tal

Adding -al to a word sometimes changes the vowel sound in a syllable before the ending.

nā' ture ⟶ năt' u ral

nā' tion ⟶ nă' tion al

Adding -al to a word sometimes changes *both* the vowel sound and the accent pattern.

rĕm' ə dy ⟶ rē mē' di al

or' ə i gin ⟶ ə rĭg' in al

Say the following words carefully, listening for an accent or a vowel change. Draw a box around the accented syllables. Place a check in the column that tells what kind of change occurs. Some words may have no change.

	Accent Change	Vowel-Sound Change	No Change
1. department ⟶ departmental	✓		
2. tide ⟶ tidal			
3. origin ⟶ original			
4. nation ⟶ national			
5. architecture ⟶ architectural			
6. secretary ⟶ secretarial			
7. option ⟶ optional			
8. nature ⟶ natural			
9. universe ⟶ universal			
10. remedy ⟶ remedial			
11. orient ⟶ oriental			

WORKSHEET 15-G

Adding the ending -al to some Latin roots changes them from nouns to adjectives.
Remember two spelling rules. Use the correct rule for the words with * or #.

*1. Drop the final e before adding an ending beginning with a vowel.

#2. Change the final y to i before adding an ending beginning with a vowel.

Noun	Adjective (Add al)	ABC Order
coast ⟶		
occasion ⟶		
person ⟶		
option ⟶		
department ⟶		
exception ⟶		
*fate ⟶		
*globe ⟶		
*spine ⟶		
*architecture ⟶		
*tide ⟶		
*nature ⟶		
*structure ⟶		
*universe ⟶		
#remedy ⟶		
#secretary ⟶		
#territory ⟶		

Now go back and write the adjectives in alphabetical order.

These three words change from *verbs* to *nouns*.

Verb	Noun (Add al)
*reverse ⟶	
*arrive ⟶	
*remove ⟶	

WORKSHEET 15-H

Review: In words such as *globe* you have to _____ _____ _____ before adding *al*.

In words such as *secretary* you have to change the _____ to _____ before adding *al*.

Write the -*al* word that fits the definition. Look for the root in the definition. Use the spelling rules from Worksheet 15-G.

1. Having to do with the Orient _____

2. Having to do with the coast _____

3. Having to do with a structure _____

4. Having to do with a globe _____

5. Having to do with a department _____

6. Having to do with nature _____

7. Having to do with music _____

8. Having to do with an accident _____

9. Having to do with a secretary _____

10. The act of removing something _____

11. The act of reversing something _____

12. The act of arriving _____

13. A person who commits crimes _____

14. Lasting for eternity _____

Proofing Practice: Two common List 15 words are misspelled in each of the sentences below. Correct them as shown.

1. The crowd was ~~frantiek~~ *frantic* when it heard about the bomb in the railroad terminel.

2. Mr. Royal is alergic to anumal hair.

3. After his arrivle in the capital city, General Kramarchik toured the hospital and the royel palace.

4. The Olympic champions were both athletik and patreotic.

5. We found gorgeous corel in the tide pools of the South Atlantick coastal reefs.

9

Fill in each blank with the correct *-al* or *-ic* word. Then complete the puzzle.

ge o graph ic   ac ro bat ic   an gel ic   pa tri o tic

en er get ic   ath let ic   ar tis tic   gi gan tic

ti dal   math e mat i cal   he ro ic   cat as troph ic

crit ic   e lec tric   min er al

1. An artist is _____. (7 Down)

2. An athlete is _____.
   (9 Down)

3. An acrobat is _____.
   (11 Across)

4. An angel is _____.
   (4 Across)

5. A catastrophe can be described as

   _____. (15 Across)

6. A hero is _____. (8 Down)

7. If something has to do with math, it is

   _____. (6 Across)

8. A patriot is _____.
   (3 Down)

9. _____s come out of mines.
   (10 Down)

10. Someone with lots of energy is said to be

    _____. (13 Across)

11. Someone who criticizes is called a

    _____. (14 Across)

12. Something that uses electricity is

    _____. (1 Down)

13. A giant is _____. (12 Across)

14. _____ means "having to do with
    the tide." (2 Down)

15. _____ means "hav-
    ing to do with geography." (5 Down)

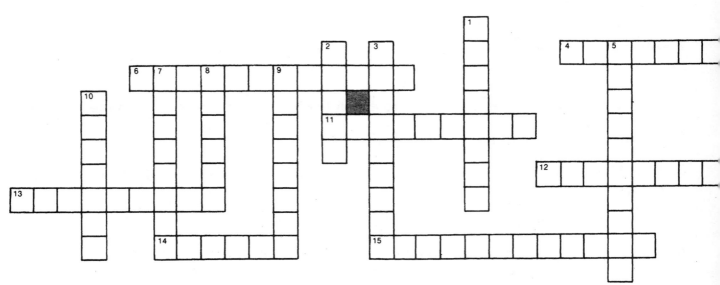

Read the following sentences and circle all the List 15 words that you can find.

1. The Atlantic and Pacific are gigantic oceans.

2. Eric Royal was a loyal and energetic legal scholar.

3. A global atomic war would be catastrophic.

4. The final trip ended with their frantic arrival at the general hospital.

5. Several of the critics thought that the vocal music was poor.

6. The coral reefs along the coastal shelf are fantastic.

7. The general had oral surgery at the dental clinic.

8. The people whom the criminal held up in the bus terminal started to panic.

9. Cedric thinks that he is allergic to garlic.

10. A local electrical storm tied up traffic in the central part of the city.

Look at List 15. Choose five words and write them in sentences below.

_____

_____

_____

_____

_____

Take out a piece of blank paper. Your teacher will dictate three of the sentences above for you to write.

You have completed the worksheets for List 15. Now it is time to check your accuracy in reading and spelling. Read and spell ten words selected by your teacher, and record your scores on the Accuracy Checklist. Work toward 90-100 percent accuracy.

When you have achieved 90-100 percent accuracy in reading, build up your reading speed. Decide on your rate goal with your teacher. Record your rate on the Proficiency Graph.

My goal for reading List 15 is _____ words per minute with two or fewer errors.

LIST 16: /ĭt/ AND /ət/ ENDINGS

-it=/ĭt/ or /et/	-et=/ĭt/ or /ət/	-ite=/ĭt/ or /ət/	-ate=/ĭt/ or /ət/	-ate=/ĭt/ and /āt/[1]
audit	*pocket	granite	*chocolate	delegate
*limit	*blanket	*favorite	*climate	*separate
*habit	*quiet	*definite	delicate	*estimate
*unit	*planet	composite	desperate	approximate
*permit	*market	hypocrite	accurate	*moderate
commit	*closet	requisite	confederate	deliberate
*deposit	bucket	exquisite	*fortunate	advocate
*benefit	*jacket	*opposite	affectionate	appropriate
prohibit	suet	indefinite	obstinate	-ate=/āt/[1]
inhabit	velvet	prerequisite	*private	isolate
inhibit	toilet		certificate	liberate
biscuit	budget		illiterate	escalate
tacit	rocket		*senate	invalidate
orbit	cricket		immaculate	abdicate
implicit	racket		pirate	vaccinate
explicit	fidget		agate	congratulate
debit	gadget			illustrate
inherit	*diet			concentrate
*credit	banquet			accumulate
profit	trumpet			accelerate
	violet			compensate
	*wallet			violate
	poet			evaporate
	*target			stimulate
	*basket			

[1]Although /āt/ is not an unaccented ending, it seems appropriate to include the words in this list with the other -ate words.
*Practical spelling words. The teacher and student should decide together how many of these words the student will be responsible for spelling.

WORKSHEET 16-A

-*it*, -*et*, -*ite*, and -*ate* are unaccented endings that say /ĭt/ or /ət/.

Review: In two- and three-syllable words, accent the first syllable. Then pronounce the first vowel as if it were a short, long, *r*-controlled, or double-vowel sound in a one-syllable word. If that doesn't make a recognizable word, accent the second syllable, and pronounce the second vowel according to its syllabic type.

Pronounce and combine the syllables to read the whole word. Then cover the divided word and practice reading the whole word. Draw a box around the accented syllable and underline the -*it*, -*et*, -*ite*, or -*ate* ending as shown.

Accent the First Syllable

_ ´   _

lim	it	limit
rack	et	racket
qui	et	quiet
or	bit	orbit
hab	it	habit
u	nit	unit
plan	et	planet
pi	rate	pirate
sen	ate	senate
pri	vate	private
ag	ate	agate
prof	it	profit
su	et	suet

_ ´   _   _

fa	vor	ite	favorite
op	po	site	opposite
ac	cur	ate	accurate
des	per	ate	desperate
def	in	ite	definite
choc	o	late	chocolate
ob	sti	nate	obstinate
es	ti	mate	estimate
del	i	cate	delicate
for	tu	nate	fortunate
hyp	o	crite	hypocrite
sep	a	rate	separate (adj.)
mod	er	ate	moderate (adj.)

Accent the Second Syllable

_   _ ´   _

in	hib	it	inhibit
in	her	it	inherit

im	plic	it	implicit
com	pos	ite	composite

The most common accent pattern in four-syllable words places the accent on the second syllable (— —′ — —).

Pronounce and combine the syllables to read these four-syllable words. Then cover the divided word and practice reading the whole word. Draw a box around the accented syllable and underline the ending as shown.

in def i nite	indefinite
il lit er ate	illiterate
cer tif i cate	certificate
de lib er ate	deliberate
pre req ui site	prerequisite

af fec tion ate	affectionate
con fed er ate	confederate
ap prox i mate	approximate
im mac u late	immaculate
con grat u late	congratulate

Unscramble these three-syllable words. If you circle the *-it*, *-et*, *-ite*, or *-ate* ending, you will know which syllable is last.

fa   ite   vor   _____

o   choc   late   _____

it   in   hab   _____

i   nite   def   _____

pos   it   de   _____

po   op   site   _____

per   ate   des   _____

lus   il   trate   _____

Find and circle the eighteen words above in the puzzle below. The words can be found in a straight line across or up and down.

```
D E L I B E R A T E C E R T I F I C A T E I
E C H M O P R E R E Q U I S I T E A N G E L
F T H M P E F I C O N F E D E R A T E N A L
I L Y A P P R O X I M A T E T O I B E F O I
N R E C O N G R A T U L A T E D E P O S I T
I L L U S T R A T E A D D I N G A N E N D E
T I N L I F A V O R I T E G B E G I N N I R
E N G A T I N H A B I T D E S P E R A T E A
W I T T E H C H O C O L A T E A V O W E L T
I N D E F I N I T E A F F E C T I O N A T E
```

WORKSHEET 16-C

Review: -ate is sometimes pronounced /ĭt/ or /ət/.

However, the ending -ate can also say /āt/. When it does, there is some stress on it. In three-syllable words, the first syllable has the stronger, or primary, accent and -ate has a slight, or secondary, accent (__' __ __').

    <u>vi</u>' o late'   violate

In four-syllable words, the second syllable has the stronger accent (__ __' __ __').

    con <u>grat</u>' u late'   congratulate

Pronounce and combine the syllables to read the whole word. Draw a box around the syllable that has the stronger accent in each word.

Three-Syllable Words

stim u late	stim̲ulate	i so late	isolate
lib er ate	liberate	con cen trate	concentrate
vac ci nate	vaccinate	ab di cate	abdicate
es ca late	escalate	il lus trate	illustrate
com pen sate	compensate	vi o late	violate

Four-Syllable Words

in val i date	in̲val̲idate
ac cum u late	accumulate
e vap or ate	evaporate
ac cel er ate	accelerate

Pronounce these words that end in -ate with both ending sounds—/āt/ and /ĭt/.

es ti mate	es̲timate	sep a rate	separate
del e gate	delegate	ad vo cate	advocate
de lib er ate	deliberate	ap prox i mate	approximate

15

WORKSHEET 16-D

Your teacher will dictate some words. Sound each one out as you write it. Then write the whole word, saying it aloud as you spell it.

	Copy	ABC Order
1. _____ et	_____	_____
2. _____ et	_____	_____
3. _____ et	_____	_____
4. _____ et	_____	_____
5. _____ ____et	_____	_____
6. _____ _____ it	_____	_____
7. _____ ____it	_____	_____
8. _____ _____ it	_____	_____
9. _____ _____ it	_____	_____
10. _____ ____it	_____	_____
11. _____ ite	_____	_____
12. _____ _____ ite	_____	_____
13. _____ _____ ____ite	_____	_____
14. _____ _____ ite	_____	_____
15. _____ _____ ite	_____	_____
16. _____ _____ ____ate	_____	_____
17. _____ _____ ate	_____	_____
18. _____ _____ ____ate	_____	_____
19. _____ ____ate	_____	_____
20. _____ _____ ____ate	_____	_____

Now go back and write the words in alphabetical order.

Review: *-it, -et, -ite,* and *-ate* are unaccented endings that say /_____/. *-ate* can also say

/_____/. Which *-ate* word above can have both sounds? _____

16

WORKSHEET 16-E

Words that end in -et, pronounced /ĭt/ or /ət/, are usually only two syllables long.

Complete these words by adding *et*. Then write the words in alphabetical order.

Add *et*	Copy	ABC Order
pock_____	_____	_____
qui_____	_____	_____
fidg_____	_____	_____
clos_____	_____	_____
velv_____	_____	_____
rock_____	_____	_____
di_____	_____	_____
mark_____	_____	_____
jack_____	_____	_____
viol_____	_____	_____

Which word above has *three* syllables?_____

Complete the following sentences with words from above.

1. Bridget had a comb in the _____ of her _____.

2. The _____ and the primrose are spring flowers.

3. Be_____ and still; please do not_____ so much while we are watching the movie.

4. Alexander needed to go on a _____ to lose weight.

5. Her _____ dress was hanging in the _____.

6. A _____ carried the spacecraft into orbit.

7. The farmers' _____ sells gigantic baskets of fruit.

WORKSHEET 16-F

Review: In two- and three-syllable words, the accent is most often on the _____ syllable.

Identify the accented syllables in the following words, and then copy the words by syllables under the correct heading. Write the accented syllables in the boxes.

unit	escalate	benefit	quiet
toilet	diet	definite	granite
liberate	vaccinate	blanket	credit
concentrate	senate	bucket	separate
violate	accurate	opposite	climate

Two-Syllable Words   Three-Syllable Words

WORKSHEET 16-G

When the ending -*ate* says /ĭt/ or /ət/, it is unaccented. The accent is on another syllable (*cli' mate*, *for' tu nate*).

When -*ate* says /āt/, it has a slight, or secondary, accent. Another syllable has a stronger accent.

Read these words. Look at the accent patterns. Then write the words under the correct heading.

un for' tu nate	stim' u late'	ac' cur ate	cli' mate
cer tif' i cate	vi' o late'	des' per ate	ac cu' mu late'
sen' ate	il' lus trate'	vac' ci nate'	con' cen trate'
af fec' tion ate	i' so late'	pi' rate	e vap' or ate'

-*ate*=/ĭt/ or /ət/   -*ate*=/āt/

_____   _____

_____   _____

_____   _____

_____   _____

_____   _____

_____   _____

_____   _____

_____   _____

Review: When -*ate* says /ĭt/ or /ət/, it is u_____.

When -*ate* says /āt/, it has a s_____ accent.

Look at the words you have written in the first column above. Write each of them under the correct heading below.

Two-Syllable Words	Three-Syllable Words	Four-Syllable Words
_____	_____	_____
_____	_____	_____
_____		_____

WORKSHEET 16-H

Write each word in the correct set of boxes, paying attention to the ending and number of syllables.

*favorite	climate	*limit	*opposite
deliberate	*quiet	prerequisite	*market
*fortunate	*benefit	inhabit	indefinite
delicate	*jacket	*planet	*habit
granite	inherit	certificate	*closet

-it

-ite

| fa | vor | ite |

1 2 3 4

-et

-ate

Review: In two- and three-syllable words, the accent is usually on the _____ syllable.

In four-syllable words, the accent is usually on the _____ syllable.

Have another student test you on spelling the starred words. They are practical spelling words.

My score: _____ words correct.

WORKSHEET 16-I

Underline the letters that say /ĭt/ or /ət/ in each of these words. Then write the words under the appropriate heading.

*clim<u>ate</u>	*quiet	rocket	*favorite
*permit	confederate	composite	*deposit
indefinite	*planet	*benefit	*moderate
*market	biscuit	*separate	deliberate
affectionate	toilet	bucket	*target
*opposite	*immediate	delicate	inhabit

-it
_____
_____
_____
_____
_____

-ite
_____
_____
_____

-et
_____
_____
_____
_____
_____
_____
_____

-ate
climate
_____
_____
_____
_____
_____
_____

Have another student test you on spelling the starred words. They are practical spelling words.

My score: _____ words correct.

Proofing Practice: Two common List 16 words are misspelled in each of the sentences below. Correct them as shown.

    crickets
1. The ~~criekits~~ in our yard raise such a rackett that it is hard to go to sleep at night.

2. Garrett found a wallett filled with Confederite money in the pirate's trash basket.

3. That agate is exquisate; maybe you should put it in your safe deposet box.

WORKSHEET 16-J

All of these words are practical spelling words that end with the /ĭt/ or /ət/ sound. Add the correct ending, *-et, -it, -ite,* or *-ate,* and copy the whole word.

Add Ending	Copy	ABC Order
1. pock_____	_____	_____
2. hab_____	_____	_____
3. perm_____	_____	_____
4. chocol_____	_____	_____
5. priv_____	_____	_____
6. favor_____	_____	_____
7. oppos_____	_____	_____
8. plan_____	_____	_____
9. sen_____	_____	_____
10. qui_____	_____	_____
11. defin_____	_____	_____
12. depos_____	_____	_____
13. blank_____	_____	_____

Now go back and write the words in alphabetical order.

Unscramble the words below and spell them correctly in the blanks and circles. All the words can be found in the list above.

T I E Q U   _ _ _ _ ◯

T E A C H C O O L   _ ◯ _ _ _ _ _ _

F A I R V O T E   _ _ _ _ _ ◯ _ _

T E N S E A   _ _ _ ◯ _ _

N E T B A L K   ◯ _ _ _ _ _ _

Unscramble the letters you have written in the circles to make another word from the list above:

_ _ _ _ _

22

WORKSHEET 16-K

All of the words below end in /ĭt/ or /ət/. Write the word that fits the definition.

desperate	definite	delicate	biscuit
immediate	prohibit	certificate	cricket
benefit	obstinate	fidget	fortunate

1. A type of bread or muffin _____

2. Something that helps; a useful aid; to help _____

3. A small leaping insect that chirps _____

4. To move nervously or restlessly _____

5. Dainty, sensitive, breakable _____

6. Stubborn _____

7. Beyond hope; causing despair _____

8. Certain, sure, clear in meaning _____

9. Right away _____

10. To forbid _____

11. Written statement that may be used as proof of some fact _____

12. Having good luck, lucky _____

Divide the words below into syllables as shown. Draw a box around the accented syllables, and pronounce the words aloud.

des‧per‧ate	immediate	benefit	definite
prohibit	obstinate	delicate	certificate
fidget	biscuit	cricket	fortunate

23

WORKSHEET 16-L

The -ate ending in all of the words below can be pronounced two ways, depending on the way the word is used.
If the word is used as a verb, the ending says /āt/.
If the word is used as a noun or an adjective, the ending says /ĭt/ or /ət/.

Fill in each blank with the correct -ate word. Each word will be used twice—once as a verb and once as a noun or an adjective.

estimate   graduate   moderate   deliberate

delegate   separate   advocate   appropriate

Verb=/āt/

1. To finish school—to
   _____

2. To take apart—to _____

3. To think about carefully—to
   _____

4. To judge the approximate size or value
   of something—to_____

5. To entrust to another; to give someone
   authority—to _____

6. To make less severe or intense—
   to _____

7. To speak in favor of; to support—
   to _____

8. To take without right—
   to _____

Noun or Adjective=/ĭt/ or /ət/

1. Someone who has finished school—a
   _____

2. An opinion or judgment about the size or
   cost of something—an _____

3. Not connected; divided—
   _____

4. A person sent with power to act for
   another—a _____

5. Thought-out; on purpose—
   _____

6. A person who speaks in favor; a sup-
   porter—an _____

7. Not extreme (adjective); someone who is
   not extreme (noun)—_____

8. Suitable—_____

WORKSHEET 16-M

Fill in each blank with a word from below. Then complete the puzzle with the words you have used.

inhabit   opposite   accurate   affectionate

granite   inherit   definite   commit

prohibit   climate   chocolate   favorite

1. If you _____ a crime, you may have to go to jail.
   (6 Across)
2. The grandchildren will _____ money when their grandfather dies.
   (12 Across)
3. *Dull* is the _____ of *shiny*.
   (2 Down)
4. Ellie's _____ ice cream flavor is _____.
   (10 Down)   (1 Across)
5. The principal tried to _____ running in the halls.
   (8 Across)
6. It is _____ that we will go tomorrow morning.
   (5 Down)
7. Margaret likes to kiss and hug people; she is very _____.
   (9 Across)
8. People who _____ the desert live in a dry _____.
   (11 Down)   (3 Down)
9. Garrett's watch is not _____; it is slow.
   (4 Down)
10. The building is made of _____.
    (7 Down)

25

Circle all the words in the story that end in *-et, -it, -ite,* or *-ate*. Write them at the bottom of the page under the appropriate headings. Write each word only once. The words may have another ending after *-et, -it, -ite,* or *-ate* (for example, *crick__ets__, inhab__ited__, delic__ately__*).

Once upon a time there lived a (confederate) soldier who was addicted to chocolate biscuits. They were his favorite food!

The soldier always carried biscuits in the pocket of his jacket. He also had a bucket full of them in his closet. When he ran out, he would immediately fidget and become desperate. He would hurry to the market and spoil his budget by spending too much money on them. His diet was limited to biscuits.

The soldier went to a doctor who said that he was definitely crazy. He had to learn to eat more moderately and appropriately. He was explicitly prohibited from eating chocolate biscuits and had to flush all the biscuits down a toilet. He was committed to a separate room where he had to be quiet and lie under a blanket whenever he was desperate for a biscuit. However, he *was* permitted to eat suet.

-et	-ate	-it
_____	*confederate*	_____
_____	_____	_____
_____	_____	_____
_____	_____	_____
_____	_____	_____
_____	_____	
_____	_____	**-ite**
_____		_____
_____		_____
_____		
_____		

WORKSHEET 16-O

Read the following sentences and circle all the List 16 words that you can find.

1. Please permit an audit of your deposit slips.

2. The velvet jacket and the blanket are in the closet.

3. I will congratulate the moderate delegate, who will be a good candidate.

4. Janet was desperate to move to a place with a milder climate because her health was delicate.

5. Emmet had to change his eating habits when he went on a diet.

6. The senate held a private meeting to discuss the debits and credits.

7. With a rocket so accurate, we may soon be able to inhabit other planets.

8. If you promise to be quiet and not to fidget, I'll give you a chocolate biscuit.

9. The fortunate player won the tennis racket at the church benefit.

10. We had to commit the general to the private unit of the mental hospital.

11. The estimate of next year's budget is only approximate.

Look at List 16. Choose five words and write them in sentences below.

_____

_____

_____

_____

_____

Take out a piece of blank paper. Your teacher will dictate three of the sentences above for you to write.

You have completed the worksheets for List 16. Now it is time to check your accuracy in reading and spelling. Read and spell ten words selected by your teacher, and record your scores on the Accuracy Checklist. Work toward 90-100 percent accuracy.

When you have achieved 90-100 percent accuracy in reading, build up your reading speed. Decide on your rate goal with your teacher. Record your rate on the Proficiency Graph.

My goal for reading List 16 is _____ words per minute with two or fewer errors.

LIST 17: MIDDLE-SYLLABLE SCHWA

a=/ə/	e=/ə/	o=/ə/	u=/ə/
*alphabet	*envelope	*chocolate	porcupine
*Canada	comedy	*absolute	insulate
pharmacist	*enemy	balcony	*calculate
*relative	*elephant	*compromise	insulin
matador	segregate	improvise	*argument
laxative	persecute	acrobat	pendulum
*permanent	complement	*innocent	instrument
metaphor	antelope	advocate	*occupy
cinnamon	congregate	hypnotize	*singular
buffalo	competent	diplomat	incubate
emphasize	correlate	suffocate	*regular
ornament	supplement	octopus	
moccasin	elevate	*alcohol	
*pharmacy	*benefit	abdomen	
sacrament	Jeremy	pantomime	
*separate	Madeline	exodus	
Melanie	Adeline	obsolete	
Agatha	execute	democrat	
Isabel	remedy	*customer	
manager		custody	
		Christopher	

*Practical spelling words. The teacher and student should decide together how many of these words the student will be responsible for spelling.

28

WORKSHEET 17-A

Review: The schwa (ə) sounds like short *u*. The schwa sound is always found in unaccented syllables. *Any vowel* can make the schwa sound. When you spell, learn to try another vowel if one does not look right.

All List 17 words have a schwa sound in the middle syllable. The schwa sound may be spelled *a, e, o,* or *u*.[1]

Write four ways to spell the following middle syllables that have the schwa sound.

First   Middle Last
Syllable Syllable Syllable

_____/trə/_____ might be spelled _*tra*_ _*tre*_ _*tro*_ _*tru*_

_____/mə/_____ might be spelled _____ _____ _____ _____

_____/nə/_____ might be spelled _____ _____ _____ _____

_____/plə/_____ might be spelled _____ _____ _____ _____

_____/tə/_____ might be spelled _____ _____ _____ _____

_____/sə/_____ might be spelled _____ _____ _____ _____

_____/prə/_____ might be spelled _____ _____ _____ _____

Review: Any vowel can make the _____ sound.

In List 17 the four vowels that make the schwa sound in the middle syllable are

_____, _____, _____, and _____.

A syllable with a schwa sound is u__ __ __ __ __ __ __ __.

Your teacher will dictate syllables containing the schwa sound. Write the four ways that these syllables can be spelled.

1. _____ _____ _____ _____

2. _____ _____ _____ _____

3. _____ _____ _____ _____

4. _____ _____ _____ _____

[1] *i* in the middle syllable will be discussed in a forthcoming book.

29

WORKSHEET 17-B

All of the words below have three syllables with an accented first syllable and an unaccented middle syllable.

The unaccented middle syllable has a schwa sound /ə/, which is spelled *a, e, o,* or *u.*

Most often the accent is on the first syllable of a three-syllable word (<u>al'</u> pha bet, <u>reg'</u> u lar).

Pronounce and combine the syllables to read the whole word. Then draw a box around the accented syllable and underline the unaccented middle syllable as shown. In the column on the right, note which vowel makes the schwa sound.

_'	/ə/	_		Middle-Syllable Schwa Spelled . . .
an	te	lope	[an]telope	e
or	na	ment	ornament	_____
ab	do	men	abdomen	_____
ab	so	lute	absolute	_____
com	ple	ment	complement	_____
dip	lo	mat	diplomat	_____
per	ma	nent	permanent	_____
el	e	vate	elevate	_____

u says /ə/ or /yə/ in an unaccented middle syllable. *u* says /yə/ after *g* or *c.*

Pronounce and combine the syllables to read the whole word. Draw a box around the accented syllable and underline the unaccented middle syllable. In the column on the right, note which sound the *u* has.

_'	_	_		Middle-Syllable *u* Says . . .
in	stru	ment	[in]strument	/ə/
por	cu	pine	porcupine	/yə/
cal	cu	late	calculate	/_/
in	su	late	insulate	/_/
in	su	lin	insulin	/_/
sin	gu	lar	singular	/_/
ar	gu	ment	argument	/_/

30

WORKSHEET 17-C

Your teacher will dictate some words. Sound each word out as you write it. Then write the whole word, saying it aloud as you spell it.

/ə/	Copy	ABC Order
1. _____na_____	_____	_____
2. _____e_____	_____	_____
3. _____pha_____	_____	_____
4. _____lo_____	_____	_____
5. _____cu_____	_____	_____
6. _____to_____	_____	_____
7. _____e_____	_____	_____
8. _____a_____	_____	_____
9. _____so_____	_____	_____
10. _____stru_____	_____	_____

Your teacher will dictate some more words. Write each word by syllables in the appropriate boxes.

a as /ə/

1.		
2.		
3.		
4.		

e as /ə/

5.		
6.		
7.		
8.		

o as /ə/

9.		
10.		
11.		
12.		

u as /yə/ or /ə/

13.		
14.		
15.		
16.		

Now go back and write the words at the top of the page in alphabetical order.

WORKSHEET 17-D

Divide the words below into syllables and write them in the appropriate boxes. Mark the long, short, and schwa vowels, and pronounce the words. You do not need to mark *r*-controlled syllables.

_ ′	ə	_	ABC Order
sŭb	jŭ	gā̄tҽ	_____
			_____
			_____
			_____
			_____
			_____
			_____
			_____
			_____
			_____
			_____
			_____
			_____
			_____

subjugate
metaphor
emphasize
elevate
persecute
acrobat
hypnotize
pendulum
improvise
suffocate
octopus
singular
execute
pharmacist

Now go back and write the words in alphabetical order.

Divide the words below into syllables as shown. Draw a box around the accented first syllable, mark the middle vowel with a schwa, and pronounce the words.

al͡cŏhol   incubate   innocent   antelope

balcony   manager   instrument   Canada

Review: The accent in these words is on the _____ syllable. The middle syllable is

u_____ and has a s_____ sound.

32

WORKSHEET 17-E

Underline the vowel that has the schwa sound in the middle syllable of each of the practical spelling words below. Then write the words in the correct column as shown.

alcohol	occupy	elephant	relative
benefit	Canada	absolute	argument
customer	alphabet	calculate	envelope

a as /ə/	*e* as /ə/	*o* as /ə/	*u* as /ə/
_____	_____	*alcohol*	_____
_____	_____	_____	_____
_____	_____	_____	_____

Fill in the vowel that spells the schwa sound in the practical spelling words below. Look up the word if necessary.

env___lope   el___phant   cust___mer   sep___rate

rel___tive   reg___lar   Can___da   occ___py

perm___nent   alc___hol   alph___bet   dipl___mat

inn___cent   arg___ment   sing___lar

Find and circle the fifteen words above in the puzzle below. The words can be found in a straight line across or up and down.

```
                                          ↓
I N N O C E N T P E R M A N E N T A S C H
W A S C A L P H A B E T D I P L O M A T O
U N D C N I S S I N G U L A R F O U N D O
N L Y U A I N A R G U M E N T U N A C C E
N T E P D D E N V E L O P E A L C O H O L
S Y L Y A E L E P H A N T S E P A R A T E
L A B C U S T O M E R E L A T I V E L E S
```

Write the leftover letters in the blanks below. Work from left to right.

__ __ __ __ __ __ __ __ __ __ __ __ __ __ __ __ __

__ __ __ __ __ __ __ __ __ __ __ __ __ __ .

33

WORKSHEET 17-F

Fill in the correct vowel for the schwa sound in these words. Look up the words if necessary. Then concentrate on the vowel that spells the schwa sound and write the whole word.

el _e_ vate   _elevate_   ins___lin   _____

el___ment   _____   arg___ment   _____

el___phant   _____   pend___lum   _____

sep___rate   _____   occ___py   _____

perm___nent   _____   calc___late   _____

pharm___cy   _____   porc___pine   _____

alc___hol   _____   dipl___mat   _____

cust___mer   _____   acr___bat   _____

dem___crat   _____   abs___lute   _____

instr___ment   _____   Can___da   _____

sing___lar   _____   alph___bet   _____

reg___lar   _____   rel___tive   _____

env___lope   _____   compr___mise   _____

ben___fit   _____   inn___cent   _____

en___my   _____   abs___lute   _____

Review: All of the words above have _____ syllables. In these words the accent is on the _____ syllable. The _____ syllable in these words is unaccented. The middle syllable in these words has a _____ sound.

WORKSHEET 17-G

Fill in each blank with the word that fits the definition. Then complete the puzzle.

1. Well qualified, capable _____ (6 Down)

2. Lasting, fixed, changeless _____ (7 Across)

3. To put to death; to carry out _____ (10 Across)

4. A sea animal with eight legs _____ (3 Down)

5. A brown spice _____ (4 Down)

6. A store where drugs are sold _____ (11 Across)

7. The opposite of a friend _____ (8 Down)

8. The belly; a part of the body _____ (5 Down)

9. A disagreement; a fight with words _____ (2 Down)

10. A soft leather slipper _____ (1 Down)

11. A person who tries to kill the bull in a bullfight _____ (1 Across)

12. A drug used by persons who have diabetes _____ (9 Across)

octopus	abdomen	moccasin	competent
enemy	argument	cinnamon	permanent
pharmacy	execute	insulin	matador

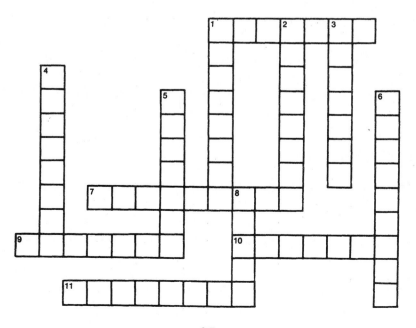

35

WORKSHEET 17-H

Complete each sentence with a word from below that makes sense.

buffalo   suffocate   alcohol   Democrat

elevate   acrobat   hypnotize   elephant

calculate   antelope   ornament   innocent

1. Anthony was _____; he did not commit the crime.

2. The water _____, the _____, and the

   _____ are animals found in Africa.

3. The _____ walked on the tightrope in the circus.

4. You can _____ the age of a tree by counting the rings in the trunk.

5. If you _____ something, you raise it.

6. Adeline decorated the banquet table with a lovely _____.

7. The _____s and Republicans have conventions to choose their presidential candidates.

8. Beer, rum, and whiskey are forms of _____.

9. If you can't get oxygen, you will _____.

10. If you put someone in a trance, you _____ them.

Proofing Practice: Two common List 17 words are misspelled in each of the sentences below. Correct them as shown.

Antelope

1. ~~Antalope,~~ water buffalo, and elephants tend to congragate near water holes.

2. The custamer who wanted to be sold insulin without a prescription argued with the pharmecist.

3. A matador often needs to be a compatent acrabat.

4. Jeremy and Melanie decided to compremise and buy one chocalate and one cinnamon doughnut.

5. I would like to emphesize that it would be disastrous to get into a fight with a porkupine or an octopus.

6. The leather moccosins Isabel bought in Canada had lovely beaded ornamants on them.

36

WORKSHEET 17-I

Read the following sentences and circle all the List 17 words that you can find.

1. Isabel and Adeline had an argument about hospital benefits.

2. The Democrats emphasized the need to compromise.

3. The pharmacist did not advocate alcohol as a remedy for her customer.

4. The octopus was not a permanent resident of the zoological gardens.

5. The porcupine does not have many enemies to persecute it.

6. Madeline used an obsolete instrument to calculate the correlations.

7. The elephant, the buffalo, and the antelope are innocent victims of human cruelty.

8. It should be mandatory for managers to execute their jobs competently.

9. Jeremy and Christopher had relatives in Canada.

10. Abdul had to elevate his leg after he fell of the porch.

11. A diplomat cannot be absolute; he or she must compromise.

Look at List 17. Choose five words and write them in sentences below.

_____

_____

_____

_____

_____

Take out a piece of blank paper. Your teacher will dictate three of the sentences above for you to write.

You have completed the worksheets for List 17. Now it is time to check your accuracy in reading and spelling. Read and spell ten words selected by your teacher, and record your scores on the Accuracy Checklist. Work toward 90-100 percent accuracy.

When you have achieved 90-100 percent accuracy in reading, build up your reading speed. Decide on your rate goal with your teacher. Record your rate on the Proficiency Graph.

My goal for reading List 17 is _____ words per minute with two or fewer errors.

LIST 18: /ənt/ AND /əns/ ENDINGS

-ant=/ənt/	*-ance*=/əns/	*-ent*=/ənt/	*-ence*=/əns/
servant	*entrance	*student	*sentence
*distant	*distance	*silent	*silence
fragrant	*balance	*absent	absence
instant	instance	*present	presence
elegant	elegance	*recent	essence
*important	*importance	rodent	*influence
defendant	hindrance	serpent	*experience
stimulant	clearance	independent	independence
dominant	brilliance	obedient	obedience
abundant	ambulance	*violent	*violence
arrogant	*insurance	*different	*difference
*significant	substance	*excellent	excellence
*ignorant	ignorance	incident	*science
constant	endurance	resident	magnificence
*infant	resistance	*frequent	audience
malignant	*appearance	decent	inference
*attendant	*attendance	*agent	preference
*vacant	*appliance	*president	reverence
*pleasant	defiance	*innocent	negligence
applicant	reliance	correspondent	correspondence
tolerant	tolerance	*intelligent	*confidence
truant	acceptance	*dependent	dependence
tenant		client	evidence
	-ancy=/əncy/	delinquent	
	hesitancy	adjacent	
	infancy		*-ency*=/əncy/
	pregnancy		agency
	vacancy		decency
			residency
			presidency

*Practical spelling words. The teacher and student should decide together how many of these words the student will be responsible for spelling.

38

WORKSHEET 18-A

The unaccented schwa ending /ənt/ can be spelled either *ant* or *ent* as in *servant* and *parent*.

The unaccented schwa ending /əns/ can be spelled either *ance* or *ence* as in *distance* and *absence*.

Write two ways to spell the following unaccented endings.

/vənt/ might be spelled   *vant*   or   *vent* .

/dəns/ might be spelled   _____ or _____ .

/təns/ might be spelled   _____ or _____ .

/ləns/ might be spelled   _____ or _____ .

/dənt/ might be spelled   _____ or _____ .

Your teacher will dictate unaccented endings that contain the sound /ənt/ or /əns/. Write two ways each ending might be spelled.

1. _____ or _____   5. _____ or _____

2. _____ or _____   6. _____ or _____

3. _____ or _____   7. _____ or _____

4. _____ or _____   8. _____ or _____

Complete the following words with *ant* or *ent*.

ant=/ənt/	*ent*=/ənt/
dis t_____	stu d_____
im por t_____	a g_____
in f_____	fre qu_____
va c_____	ex cel l_____
at ten d_____	pres i d_____
pleas _____	pres _____
sig nif i c_____	in tel li g_____

WORKSHEET 18-B

-*ant* and -*ent* are unaccented endings that say /ənt/.
In two-syllable words with -*ant* or -*ent* in the second syllable, the accent is on the first syllable (__ˊ__).

In the words below, pronounce and combine the syllables to read the whole word. Then draw a box around the accented syllable and underline the /ənt/ syllable as shown.

__ˊ __

ser	vant	servant
dis	tant	distant
fra	grant	fragrant
in	stant	instant
va	cant	vacant
tru	ant	truant

__ˊ __

stu	dent	student
si	lent	silent
ab	sent	absent
fre	quent	frequent
pres	ent	present
ser	pent	serpent

In three-syllable words, the accent is most often on the first syllable (__ˊ __ __).

__ˊ __ __

el	e	gant	elegant
stim	u	lant	stimulant
dom	i	nant	dominant
ar	ro	gant	arrogant

__ˊ __ __

vi	o	lent	violent
res	i	dent	resident
neg	li	gent	negligent
ev	i	dent	evident

If a three-syllable word has a prefix, root, and suffix, the accent is often on the root in the second syllable (__ __ˊ __).

__ __ˊ __

de	fen	dant	defendant
at	ten	dant	attendant
im	por	tant	important

__ __ˊ __

de	pen	dent	dependent
de	lin	quent	delinquent
ad	ja	cent	adjacent

40

WORKSHEET 18-C

-ance and *-ence* are unaccented endings that say /əns/.

In the words below, pronounce and combine the syllables. Then draw a box around the accented syllable, and underline the letters that make the /əns/ sound.

__ ´   __

en	trance	e̲n̲trance
bal	ance	balance
sub	stance	substance
clear	ance	clearance
dis	tance	distance
in	stance	instance

__ ´   __

sen	tence	sentence
es	sence	essence
si	lence	silence
sci	ence	science
ab	sence	absence
pres	ence	presence

__ ´   __   __

am	bu	lance	a̲m̲bulance
tol	er	ance	tolerance
el	e	gance	elegance
ar	ro	gance	arrogance
vi	o	lence	violence
rev	er	ence	reverence
neg	li	gence	negligence
dif	fer	ence	difference

__   __ ´   __

re	li	ance	reliance
en	dur	ance	endurance
at	ten	dance	attendance
im	por	tance	importance

Review: In two- and three-syllable words, the accent is most often on the _____ syllable.

If a three-syllable word has a prefix, root, and suffix, the accent is often on the _____ syllable.

41

WORKSHEET 18-D

Your teacher will dictate some words. Sound each word out as you write it syllable by syllable. Then write the whole word, saying it aloud as you write it.

1. _____ ____ant   _____

2. _____ ____ance   _____

3. _____ ____ent   _____

4. _____ ____ence   _____

5. _____ _____ ance   _____

6. _____ _____ant   _____

7. _____ _____ ____ant _____

8. _____ _____ ____ant _____

9. _____ ____ent   _____

10. _____ _____ ence   _____

Your teacher will dictate some more words. Write each word by syllables in the appropriate boxes.

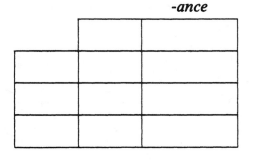

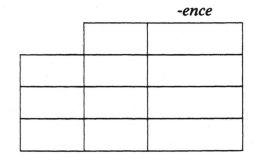

42

WORKSHEET 18-E

In the following words, identify the accented syllable, and then copy the words by syllables under the correct heading. Write the accented syllables in the boxes.

significant	absence	tolerant
client	different	abundant
confidence	magnificent	entrance
intelligence	evidence	agent
endurance	excellent	reliance
dependent	decent	intelligent

Accent the First Syllable

Accent the First Syllable

Accent the Second Syllable

Accent the Second Syllable

43

WORKSHEET 18-F

Write the practical spelling words below under the appropriate headings.

important	recent	insurance	distance
president	instant	attendance	attendant
confidence	ignorant	different	violence
frequent	appliance	experience	influence

-ant

_____

_____

_____

_____

-ance

_____

_____

_____

_____

-ent

_____

_____

_____

_____

-ence

_____

_____

_____

_____

Add the correct ending (*-ant, -ent, -ance,* or *-ence*) to make a word from List 18. Look up the word if necessary.

inf_____   stud_____   import_____

vac_____   sil_____   sci_____

appear_____   influ_____   viol_____

attend_____   differ_____   import_____

Review: In two- and three-syllable words, the accent is usually on the _____ syllable.

In four-syllable words, the accent is usually on the _____ syllable.

WORKSHEET 18-G

Learn this spelling generalization:

-*ant* becomes -*ance* (*distant* ←——→ *distance*)

-*ent* becomes -*ence* (*silent* ←——→ *silence*)

Change the adjectives that end in /ənt/ into nouns that end in /əns/ and vice versa.

Adjective -*ant*	←——→	Noun -*ance*		Adjective -*ent*	←——→	Noun -*ence*
distant		_____		_____		silence
ignorant		_____		_____		absence
important		_____		_____		presence
_____		fragrance		independent		_____
_____		elegance		obedient		_____
_____		significance		violent		_____
tolerant		_____		_____		difference
defiant		_____		_____		excellence
reliant		_____		_____		convenience
_____		instance		innocent		_____
_____		abundance		intelligent		_____
_____		attendance		confident		_____
brilliant		_____		_____		correspondence

On this page, words ending in *ant* or *ent* are a_____.

Words ending in *ance* or *ence* are n_____.

Unscramble these three-syllable words.

dence con fi   _ _ _ [   ] _ _ _ _ _ _

ap ance pear   _ _ _ _ _ _ [   ]

pen de dent   [   ] _ _ _ _ _ _ _

Now make another word from the three syllables in boxes. _ _ _ _ _ _ _ _ _

45

WORKSHEET 18-H

If you hear a hard *c* or *g* before an /ənt/ or /əns/ ending, the ending begins with *a* (*arrogant, vacant*).
If you hear a soft *c* or *g* before an /ənt/ or /əns/ ending, the ending begins with *e* (*decent, agent*).

Read these words and write them under the appropriate heading.

elegant	agent	arrogant	significant
decent	vacant	applicant	recent
innocent	adjacent	negligence	intelligent

Hard *c* or *g*	Soft *c* or *g*
1. _____	1. _____
2. _____	2. _____
3. _____	3. _____
4. _____	4. _____
5. _____	5. _____
	6. _____
	7. _____

This sentence will help you remember how to spell two very common /ənt/ words. Copy the sentence by filling in the blanks.

An import<u>ant</u> <u>ant</u> pays a diffe<u>rent</u> <u>rent</u>.

An_____ ant pays a _____ rent.

An _____ _____ pays a _____ _____.

An _____ _____ _____ _____ _____

_____ .

Review: Two ways to spell /ənt/ are _____ and _____ .

Two ways to spell /əns/ are _____ and _____ .

/ənt/ and /əns/ are un__ __ __ __ __ __ __ __ endings that have the s__ __ __ __ sound.

46

WORKSHEET 18-I

Some /ənt/ words have a noun form that sounds like /əncy/ and is spelled either *ency* or *ancy*. Change the words below to this noun form.

ent ⟶ ency
ant ⟶ ancy

Noun	Noun	Adjective	Noun
agent	*agency*	hesitant	_____
infant	_____	decent	_____
resident	_____	pregnant	_____
president	_____	vacant	_____

Fill in each blank with the correct /əncy/ word. The italicized word is your clue.

1. I noticed some _____ in Nancy's look; she was *hesitant* about going alone.

2. The apartment rental *agent* had worked in the _____ for ten years.

3. Most *infants* seem happy; _____ seems to be an untroubled time.

4. The medical *resident* had finished two years of her _____ in the hospital.

5. The *president* holds the _____ for a four-year term.

6. He seems to be a *decent* fellow; he had the _____ to call and tell us that he was going to be late.

7. Tina gained only twenty pounds while she was *pregnant* and felt healthy during all of her _____.

8. There is a _____ in the apartment building next to the *vacant* lot.

List the three-syllable words that you wrote in the blanks above:

_____, _____, _____,

_____, _____.

List the four-syllable words that you wrote in the blanks above:

_____, _____, _____.

47

WORKSHEET 18-J

Most -*ant* words are either adjectives or nouns. Many of the -*ant* nouns mean "a person who . . . ."
Write the correct word from below next to its definition.

lieutenant	inhabitant	servant	accountant
assailant	sergeant	defendant	descendant
applicant	truant	occupant	attendant

1. A person who *serves* others ___*servant*___

2. A person who is *defended* in a trial _____

3. A person who *attends* to things _____

4. A person who *applies* for a job _____

5. A person who *inhabits* a place _____

6. A person who is *descended* from someone _____

7. A person who *occupies* a place _____

8. A person who *accounts* for the finances of a business _____

9. A person who skips school _____

10. A person who attacks someone _____

11. Persons who have military positions _____ and

_____

Proofing Practice: Two common List 18 words are misspelled in each of the sentences below. Correct them as shown.

1. Ms. Torrance teaches an ~~excellant~~ *excellent* science course with frequent field trips to observe

   rodents and serpants.

2. The secret service agents guard the presidant at all public appearences.

3. I have evidence to show that the job applicant is an inteligent and desent person.

4. I wish that you would be less arrogent and more tolerant of people with differant

   opinions.

5. If the truent's school attendence does not improve, he will be sent to a residence for

   delinquents.

WORKSHEET 18-K

Change the italicized words from nouns to adjectives or from adjectives to nouns to fit the sentences. Then complete the puzzle.

Remember: Adjective ←——→ Noun
             -ent ←——→ -ence
             -ant ←——→ -ance

1. When the teacher asked for *silence,* the class became _____. (5 Down)

2. A rose is a *fragrant* flower; I like its _____. (1 Down)

3. Fido went to *obedience* school to learn to be _____. (4 Down)

4. If you are *absent* too much, the teacher will send an _____ slip home. (10 Across)

5. It is very *important* that you get all your shots; I cannot overemphasize the

   _____ of that. (8 Across)

6. If you see a movie with *violence* in it, do you become _____? (9 Across)

7. They tried to hike to a *distant* hill, but they did not make it; it was too great a

   _____. (7 Across)

8. There was not much *difference* between Florence and Patience; the twins were hardly

   _____ at all. (6 Down)

9. Lawrence knew he was *innocent,* but it was hard to prove his _____ in court. (2 Down)

10. Ellie and Garrett are good _____s; their *correspondence* is interesting. (3 Across)

WORKSHEET 18-L

Read the following sentences and circle all the List 18 words that you can find.

1. The innocent defendant has no confidence in his lawyer.

2. In this instance, it is important that each student makes an independent decision.

3. The president had evidence that the secret agent was present at the hearing.

4. There is a significant difference between delinquent and decent behavior.

5. The recent violence in the Middle East is a hindrance to world peace.

6. The client's preference is for term insurance.

7. The parking attendant was arrogant and defiant.

8. The silence in the vacant house was evidence that no one lived there.

9. The appearance of the ghost on stage made the audience shudder with fear.

10. Clarence learned about rodents and serpents in science class.

11. With her experience Ms. Clement should be able to get an excellent job.

Look at List 18. Choose five words and write them in sentences below.

_____

_____

_____

_____

_____

Take out a piece of blank paper. Your teacher will dictate three of the sentences above for you to write.

You have completed the worksheets for List 18. Now it is time to check your accuracy in reading and spelling. Read and spell ten words selected by your teacher, and record your scores on the Accuracy Checklist. Work toward 90-100 percent accuracy.
When you have achieved 90-100 percent accuracy in reading, build up your reading speed. Decide on your rate goal with your teacher. Record your rate on the Proficiency Graph.

My goal for reading List 18 is _____ words per minute with two or fewer errors.

LIST 19: UNACCENTED ENDINGS *-ive*, *-ice*, *-ace*, *-ine*, AND *-ain*

-ive=/ĭv/	*-ice, -ace*=/ĭs/ or /əs/	*-ine, -ain*=/ĭn/ or /ən/	*-ine*=/ēn/
*active	*office	*engine	sardine
massive	*service	destine	*machine
motive	*justice	doctrine	marine
captive	*practice	famine	chlorine
*relative	*notice	*discipline	*routine
elective	novice	*examine	vaccine
productive	crevice	*masculine	Pauline
*positive	jaundice	*feminine	*magazine
laxative	apprentice	*determine	mezzanine
*detective	accomplice	genuine	*gasoline
passive	*prejudice	*medicine	submarine
*expensive	cowardice	*imagine	
sensitive	*surface	*captain	
repulsive	*furnace	*curtain	
*attractive	Wallace	fountain	
*negative	terrace	*mountain	
native	preface	villain	
respective	menace	*bargain	
fugitive		chaplain	
		*certain	
		chieftain	

*Practical spelling words. The teacher and student should decide together how many of these words the student will be responsible for spelling.

51

Find and circle as many endings from Book 3 as you can: *-al, -it, -et, -ant, -ent, -ic, -ite, -ate, -ance,* *-ence, -ive, -ice, -ine, -ain, -ace.*

An Ethical Alternative

Important Notice to Members

consistent quality and excellence

Experience the difference

Worldwide Acceptance Where You Do Business Most

Genuine Porcelain Musical Figurine

CHEAP CARPET

immediate delivery

favorite way

Gas Furnace

The immortal love story of a tragic figure

CREDIT OR CASH

BOOK SERVICE

-ive is an unaccented ending that says /ĭv/.

In the words below, pronounce and combine the syllables to read the whole words. Then draw a box around the accented syllable and underline the *-ive* syllable as shown. Note the accent pattern code.

⎯́	⎯	
ac	tive	ac̲tive
mas	sive	massive
mo	tive	motive
na	tive	native
cap	tive	captive
pas	sive	passive

⎯́	⎯	⎯	
rel	a	tive	relative
pos	i	tive	positive
sen	si	tive	sensitive
neg	a	tive	negative
lax	a	tive	laxative
fu	gi	tive	fugitive

⎯	⎯́	⎯	
re	pul	sive	repulsive
at	trac	tive	attractive
re	spec	tive	respective
de	tec	tive	detective
pro	duc	tive	productive
ex	pen	sive	expensive
e	lec	tive	elective

Review: In a two-syllable word, the accent is usually on the _____ syllable.

In a three-syllable word, the accent is usually on the _____ syllable.

In a three-syllable word that has a prefix, a root, and a suffix, the accent is often on the

_____ syllable.

WORKSHEET 19-C

-*ice* and -*ace* are unaccented syllables that say /ĭs/ or /əs/.
-*ine* and -*ain* are unaccented syllables that say /ĭn/ or /ən/.

In the words below, pronounce and combine the syllables to read the whole words. Then draw a box around the accented syllable and underline the -*ice, -ace, -ine,* or -*ain* syllable as shown. Note the accent pattern code.

__'   __

of	fice	office
jus	tice	justice
nov	ice	novice
crev	ice	crevice
prac	tice	practice

__'   __

sur	face	surface
men	ace	menace
fur	nace	furnace
ter	race	terrace
pref	ace	preface

__'   __   __

prej	u	dice	prejudice
cow	ar	dice	cowardice

__   __'   __

ac	com	plice	accomplice
ap	pren	tice	apprentice

__'   __

en	gine	engine
fam	ine	famine
doc	trine	doctrine
des	tine	destine

__'   __

foun	tain	fountain
bar	gain	bargain
cur	tain	curtain
vil	lain	villain

__'   __   __

mas	cu	line	masculine
fem	i	nine	feminine
med	i	cine	medicine
dis	ci	pline	discipline

__   __'   __

im	ag	ine	imagine
de	ter	mine	determine
ex	am	ine	examine

54

WORKSHEET 19-D

The ending -ine is usually unaccented and says /ĭn/ or /ĕn/ as in *engine*.
-ine can also be an accented ending that says /ēn/ as in *magazine*.
In three-syllable words, the ending -ine, pronounced /en/, has a secondary accent and the first syllable has a primary accent.

In the words below, pronounce and combine the syllables to read the whole words. Note the accent pattern code, and draw a box around the syllable with the primary accent.

-ine=/ēn/

_____   _____ ´

sar	dine	sar[dine]
ma	chine	machine
ma	rine	marine
rou	tine	routine
vac	cine	vaccine

_____ ´   _____   _____ ´

mag	a	zine	[mag]azine
mez	za	nine	mezzanine
gas	o	line	gasoline
sub	ma	rine	submarine

Match the syllables to make real words. Say each word aloud as you write it.

ac	lain	_____	cur	tive	_____
nov	tive	_____	na	ine	_____
en	ice	_____	fam	tain	_____
vil	gine	_____	men	ace	_____

Reorder the syllables to make a recognizable word. If you circle the ending, you will know which syllable is last.

spec re	tive	_____	cine i	med	_____
rine ma	sub	_____	mag zine	a	_____
ine u	gen	_____	pul sive	re	_____
a rel	tive	_____	ter de	mine	_____
cu mas	line	_____	line o	gas	_____

Circle the words above that end in /ēn/.

WORKSHEET 19-E

Your teacher will dictate some words. Sound each word out as you write it syllable by syllable. Then write the whole word, saying it aloud as you spell it.

		Copy	ABC Order
1. _____ _____ive		_____	_____
2. _____ _____ive		_____	_____
3. _____ ___ _____ive		_____	_____
4. _____ ___ _____ive		_____	_____
5. _____ _____ice		_____	_____
6. _____ _____ ice		_____	_____
7. _____ _____ace		_____	_____
8. _____ ine		_____	_____
9. _____ ___ _____ine		_____	_____
10. _____ _____ _____ine		_____	_____
11. _____ ___ _____ine		_____	_____
12. _____ _____ain		_____	_____
13. _____ _____ine		_____	_____
14. _____ ___ _____ine		_____	_____

Now go back and write the words in alphabetical order.

These words end with *-ive, -ice,* or *-ine.* Add the correct ending; then copy the whole word.

at trac t_____   _____

re spec t_____   _____

no t_____   _____

ex a m_____   _____

gen u _____   _____

im a g_____   _____

WORKSHEET 19-F

In the following words, draw a box around the accented syllable, and then copy the words by syllables under the correct heading. Write the accented syllables in the boxes.

[na]tive	positive	sardine	productive
machine	mountain	negative	detective
office	masculine	expensive	routine
menace	discipline	engine	attractive
marine	medicine	respective	vaccine

Two-Syllable Words   Three-Syllable Words

na	tive

WORKSHEET 19-G

-ine sometimes says /ĭn/ or /ən/ as in *engine*.

-ine sometimes says /ēn/ as in *magazine*.

Write the words below under the correct heading.

marine	*medicine	*examine	Pauline
doctrine	*gasoline	chlorine	*engine
genuine	*machine	*determine	*masculine
sardine	*discipline	*magazine	*feminine
submarine	*routine	vaccine	*imagine

-ine=/ĭn/ or /ən/	-ine=/ēn/
1. _____	1. _____
2. _____	2. _____
3. _____	3. _____
4. _____	4. _____
5. _____	5. _____
6. _____	6. _____
7. _____	7. _____
8. _____	8. _____
9. _____	9. _____
10. _____	10. _____

Review: -ine is unaccented when it says /_____/.

-ine is accented when it says /_____/.

Have another student test you on spelling the starred words. They are practical spelling words.

My score: _____ words correct.

WORKSHEET 19-H

The endings -*ine* and -*ain* occur in unaccented syllables and say /ĭn/ or /ən/.

Add *ain* or *ine* to complete the common words below. Look the words up in a dictionary if necessary. Copy the words; then write them in alphabetical order.

Add *ine* or *ain*	Copy	ABC Order
*eng_____	_____	_____
*capt_____	_____	_____
*curt_____	_____	_____
*femin_____	_____	_____
*exam_____	_____	_____
vill_____	_____	_____
*barg_____	_____	_____
*cert_____	_____	_____
*mascul_____	_____	_____
genu_____	_____	_____
*discipl_____	_____	_____
*mount_____	_____	_____
*determ_____	_____	_____
fount_____	_____	_____

Have another student test you on spelling the starred words. They are practical spelling words.

My score: _____ words correct.

Find and circle all of the words above in the puzzle below. The words can be found in a straight line across or up and down.

```
D I S C I P L I N E M A S C U L I N E C
E E C A P T A I N X A H V E Q A E Z I U
T N C L F O U N T A I N B R G J I P D R
E G E N U I N E N M O U N T A I N G W T
V I L L A I N U D I M C B A R G A I N A
I N D E T E R M I N E K K I H T F B J I
L E F E M I N I N E X E O N R L Y F S N
```

59

WORKSHEET 19-I

The unaccented endings *-ice* and *-ace* say /ĭs/ or /əs/.

Write the words below under the correct heading.

office	furnace	practice	notice
surface	justice	service	menace
preface	cowardice	terrace	prejudice

ice=/ĭs/ or /əs/

1. _____

2. _____

3. _____

4. _____

5. _____

6. _____

7. _____

-ace=/ĭs/ or /əs/

1. _____

2. _____

3. _____

4. _____

5. _____

The word *police* is an exception. Is the ending accented or unaccented? _____ Does the ending say /ĭs/, /əs/, or /ēs/? /_____/

Write these practical spelling words from List 19 in the appropriate boxes below. Be sure to pay careful attention to the spelling.

active	service	practice	negative	gasoline
relative	machine	expensive	engine	routine
office	furnace	surface	medicine	magazine

-ive

-ine

-ace

-ice

Write the words below under the correct headings. Most of the words are practical spelling words. Learn them well.

gasoline	routine	bargain
masculine	genuine	sardine
villain	curtain	imagine
famine	vaccine	certain

-ine=/ēn/	-ine=/ĭn/ or /ən/	-ain=/ĭn/ or /ən/
_____	_____	_____
_____	_____	_____
_____	_____	_____
_____	_____	_____

Fill in each blank with the *-ine* or *-ain* word that fits the definition.

1. A kind of small fish preserved in oil _____
2. A fixed and regular method of doing things; a habit _____
3. Opposite of feminine _____
4. A good deal; an agreement to trade _____
5. Medicine to prevent sickness, usually given as a shot _____
6. A fuel for cars _____
7. Sure; fixed; settled _____
8. Real; not fake _____
9. To use your imagination _____
10. Fabric over or around a window _____
11. The evil person in a story _____
12. A lack of food; a time of starvation _____

WORKSHEET 19-K

Fill in the blanks with the correct words. Then complete the puzzle. The starred words are practical spelling words. Be sure you learn how to spell them.

1. The bandits held him _____ for ten days.
   (5 Across)
2. The _____ solved the crime before the police did.
   (11 Across)
3. The diamonds were twice as _____ as the pearls.
   (6 Down)
4. Several of my _____s live in Florida.
   (4 Across)
5. Jamal is quite _____. He never does anything active.
   (2 Across)
6. The boulder was so _____ that it took two bulldozers to move it.
   (10 Across)
7. Was the _____ for the crime revenge or profit?
   (9 Across)
8. Bernice is quite _____. She never sits down.
   (1 Across)
9. Are your eyes _____ to light?
   (3 Down)
10. Mona Lisa was an _____ woman; many people find her pleasing.
    (1 Down)
11. Don't be so _____. Give us some _____ help.
    (8 Across)   (7 Across)

*positive   detective   attractive   *relative   captive   motive

massive   *sensitive   *expensive   *negative   *passive   *active

62

WORKSHEET 19-L

Write the words below next to their definitions.

novice   apprentice   crevice   accomplice

menace   terrace   mezzanine   chlorine

preface   jaundice

1. A threat; to threaten   _____

2. A low story between two higher stories of a
   building, often forming a balcony   _____

3. A flat, raised piece of land; a raised level   _____

4. A greenish-yellow gas used to purify the water in
   swimming pools   _____

5. A disease that causes yellowing of the skin, eyes,
   and body fluids   _____

6. A beginner; one who is new at what he or she is
   doing   _____

7. A person who is learning a trade, profession, or
   art   _____

8. A narrow split or crack   _____

9. A person who shares in the guilt for a crime   _____

10. An introduction to a book   _____

Unscramble the words below and spell them correctly in the blanks and circles. All the words can be found in the list above.

F R E E C A P   _ O O _ _ O _

I N C O V E   _ _ O _ O _

A N D J U I C E   _ _ _ _ _ O _ O

Unscramble the letters you have written in the circles to make another word from the list above:

_ _ _ _ _ _

63

WORKSHEET 19-M

Read these paragraphs. Underline the words that end with *-ive -ice, -ine,* and *-ain.* Note that some words have a suffix after the ending pattern.

I imagine that the doctor has an active practice in internal medicine. I notice that he routinely examines people and gives them vaccines. If a negative reaction occurs, the person is probably sensitive to the medicine.

Geraldine was a novice detective on the police force, but she was perceptive in most matters. She told the captain that the marine must have had an accomplice who was a machine operator and a native of that mountainous area.

Now copy the words you underlined under the correct heading. Write each word only once.

-ine as /ĭn/ or /ən/	*-ine* as /ēn/	*-ice* as /ĭs/ or /əs/
_____	_____	_____
_____	_____	_____
_____	_____	_____
-ive as /ĭv/	_____	
_____	_____	*-ice* as /ēs/
_____	*-ain* as /ĭn/ or /ən/	_____
_____	_____	
_____	_____	
_____		

Proofing Practice: Two common List 19 words are misspelled in each of the sentences below. Correct them as shown.

determine
1. Pauline was unable to ~~determin~~ if the diamonds in the expensive necklace were genuin.

2. The captin was taken captiv during the riots in his native country.

3. The detektive was certain that Wallace had been an accomplace to the crime.

Read the following sentences and circle all the List 19 words that you can find.

1. The marine was held captive by the natives.

2. Pauline read a magazine in the chaplain's office.

3. The solar-powered engine was an expensive machine.

4. Did you notice the gasoline fumes around the furnace?

5. Ask the service station attendant to examine the car's engine.

6. The police detective brought the villain to justice.

7. Massive doses of the medicine cured the jaundice.

8. The apprentice needed to practice running the office machines.

9. The velvet curtains were certainly no bargain.

10. The captain was certain that he could climb to the top of the mountain.

11. Mr. Wallace was unable to determine whether the pearl was genuine.

Look at List 19. Choose five words and write them in sentences below.

_____

_____

_____

_____

_____

Take out a piece of blank paper. Your teacher will dictate three of the sentences above for you to write.

You have completed the worksheets for List 19. Now it is time to check your accuracy in reading and spelling. Read and spell ten words selected by your teacher, and record your scores on the Accuracy Checklist. Work toward 90-100 percent accuracy.

When you have achieved 90-100 percent accuracy in reading, build up your reading speed. Decide on your rate goal with your teacher. Record your rate on the Proficiency Graph.

My goal for reading List 19 is _____ words per minute with two or fewer errors.

REVIEW: LISTS 15-19

* final	* limit	* envelope	* vacant
captive	panic	velvet	diplomat
* insurance	* terrific	* fortunate	porcupine
* violent	* captain	removal	* definite
* relative	fountain	oral	* permit
comedy	* important	incubate	garlic
toilet	octopus	* attendance	* gigantic
moderate	* calculate	* different	villain
* several	* chocolate	accurate	inhabit
* arrival	* benefit	kangaroo	* ignorant
* Atlantic	* positive	vaccine	granite
* silent	* fantastic	certificate	* occupy
* frequent	* magazine	* picnic	* notice
* furnace	* justice	* hospital	* pocket
* permanent	* entrance	* elastic	* diet
* alcohol	* absent	* practice	reversal
vaccinate	* singular	* president	* gasoline
* influence	concentrate	* sentence	* certain
* plastic	* market	* innocent	ambulance
sarcastic	* opposite	democrat	* present
* masculine	* natural	* prejudice	* feminine

*Practical spelling words. The teacher and student should decide together how many of these words the student will be responsible for spelling.

ACROSS
1. last (15)*
5. place where sick people are treated (15)
12. out loud; having to do with the mouth (15)
13. you order dinner from this (6)
14. color between white and black
15. the taking away of something (15)
16. a skeleton is made of many of these
18. continent across the Atlantic
20. grand; regal; lordly (7)
21. United States (abbrev.)
23. to tangle; to growl
25. _____ and tuck; to pinch
28. a person who gets information secretly
29. first four vowels
32. southern state; capital is Montgomery
35. prefix meaning "together; with" (10)
37. sounds the same as oar; either— _____
38. one who rents (18)
40. Connecticut (abbrev.)
41. Washington (abbrev.)
42. opposite of an exit (18)
44. friend; chum
45. _____ and fro; sounds the same as two
46. dull; insensitive (14)
49. missing in action (abbrev.)
50. to lose; to put in the wrong place (10)
51. opposite of give
52. a longing; also, money unit in Japan
53. took away (13)
56. a fight between two people (8)
59. opposite of friend (17)
60. fast, _____, fastest (11)

DOWN
1. lucky (16)
2. anger
3. word that tells who or what something is
4. orally (14)
5. to assist; aid
6. opposite of off
7. prefix meaning "below, under" (9)
8. lacking knowledge (18)
9. high pitched voice; soprano
10. Alcoholics Anonymous (abbrev.)
11. harp used in ancient Greece
13. Chinese leader (1949-1976)
17. once up_____ _____ time
19. extrasensory perception (abbrev.)
22. quiet (18)
24. New York City (abbrev.)
26. to tell a story without words (17)
27. country north of U.S. (17)
28. South America (abbrev.)
30. central U.S. state; capital is Des Moines (8)
31. same as 12 across (15)
33. to keep out
34. mountain (abbrev.)
36. to live in (17)
39. opposite of credit (16)
43. opposite of tragedy (17)
44. a kind of nut (1)
47. used for sliding down hills in snow
48. a flying creature covered with feathers
49. to imitate without speaking
51. a valuable stone
54. opposite of off
55. two letters of have used in contractions
57. electrical engineer (abbrev.)
58. Lillian Russell (initials)

*The number in parentheses after clues tells which list the word comes from.

67

SUMMARY OF ACCENT PATTERNS

Accented Syllable—An accented syllable is pronounced as if it were a one-syllable word with a clear vowel sound according to its syllabic type *(ac′ tive, com plete′, ser′ vant, loy′ al).*

Unaccented Syllable—An unaccented syllable is pronounced with a schwa /ə/ or short-*i* /ĭ/ vowel sound regardless of its syllabic type *(rib′ bon, op′ po site, in de pen′ dent).*

Accent Patterns—Learning to place the accent on the proper syllable will help you recognize most multisyllabic words. The accent patterns below will help you determine which syllable in a word is accented.

Primary Accent—A strong stress on a syllable in a multisyllabic word.

Secondary Accent—A weaker stress on a syllable in a multisyllabic word.

General Guideline—In two- and three-syllable words, accent the first syllable. Then pronounce the first vowel as if it were a short, long, *r*-controlled, or double-vowel sound in a one-syllable word. If that doesn't make a recognizable word, accent the second syllable, and pronounce the second vowel according to its syllabic type.

Accent Patterns for Two-Syllable Words

1. Accent on the first syllable (__′ __)
   Most two-syllable words have the accent on the first syllable *(fi′ nal, hop′ ping, stu′ dent).*
2. Accent on the second syllable (__ __′)
   Two-syllable words that have a prefix in the first syllable and a root in the second syllable are usually accented on the second syllable *(ex tend′, con fuse′).*
3. Accent on either the first or second syllable (__′ __ or __ __′)
   If a word can function as both noun and verb, the noun is accented on the prefix *(con′ duct)* and the verb is accented on the root *(con duct′).*

Accent Patterns for Three-Syllable Words

1. Accent on the first syllable (__′ __ __)
   Most often the accent is on the first syllable of a three-syllable word. The unaccented middle syllable has a schwa sound *(al′ pha bet, reg′ u lar, choc′ o late).*
2. Accent on the second syllable (__ __′ __)
   This pattern often occurs in words that contain a prefix, root, and suffix. The accent is on the root in the second syllable *(pre sent′ ing, re sis′ tance, de tec′ tive).*

Accent Patterns for Four-Syllable Words (__ __′ __ __)

1. The most common accent pattern in four-syllable words places the accent on the second syllable *(in tel′ li gence, sig nif′ i cant).*

Special Accent Patterns for Words of Three or More Syllables

Accent patterns for words longer than two syllables are often governed by a specific ending pattern or an unaccented vowel.

1. Accent with the ending *-ic*
   Accent the syllable just before the ending *-ic (fran′ tic, e las′ tic, en er get′ ic, char ac ter is′ tic).*

2. Accent with the ending *-ate* /āt/
   In three-syllable words, the first syllable has a primary accent and *-ate* has a secondary accent *(vi′ o late′).*

   In four-syllable words, the second syllable has a primary accent and *-ate* has a secondary accent *(con grat′ u late′).*

3. Accent with schwa endings
   Schwa endings (and schwa syllables) are never accented. The accent falls on another syllable in the word *(pleas′ ant, in′ no cent, ex ter′ nal, ap pren′ tice).*

ACCURACY CHECKLIST
Megawords 3, Lists 15-19

Student _____

Record accuracy score as a fraction: $\dfrac{\text{\# correct}}{\text{\# attempted}}$

List	Examples	Check Test Scores Date:		Reading			Spelling		
		Reading	Spelling						
15. /əl/ and /ĭk/ Endings *-al, -ic*	eternal athletic								
16. /ĭt/ and /ət/ Endings *-it, -et, -ite, -ate*	audit closet opposite private								
17. Middle-Syllable Schwa *a, e, o, u*	antelope chocolate								
18. /ənt/ and /əns/ Endings *-ant, -ance, -ent, -ence*	important balance different absence								
19. Unaccented Endings *-ive, -ice, -ace, -ine, -ain*	examine sensitive								
Review: Lists 15-19									

PROFICIENCY GRAPH

Student_____

Goal_____

●————● Words Read Correctly

×————× Errors

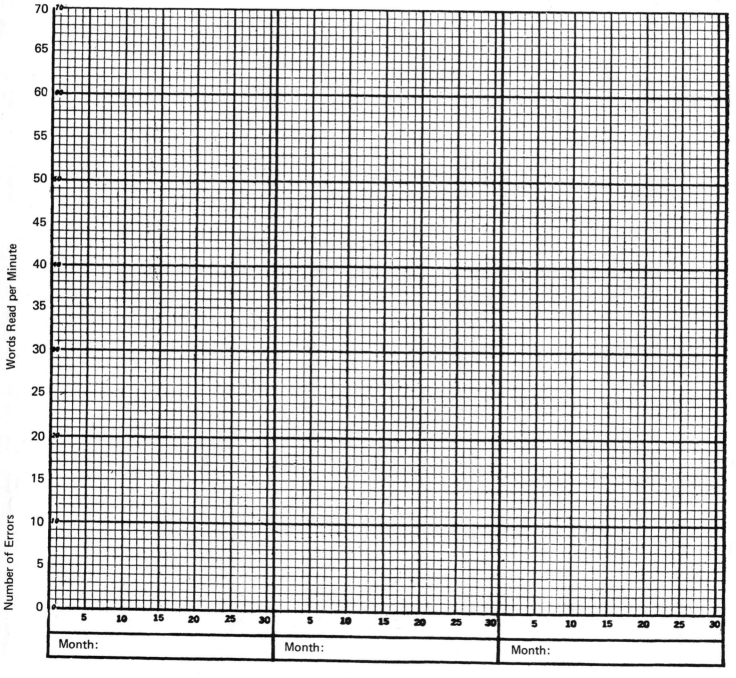

Calendar Days

71

PROFICIENCY GRAPH

Student _____

Goal _____

●————● Words Read Correctly

✕————✕ Errors

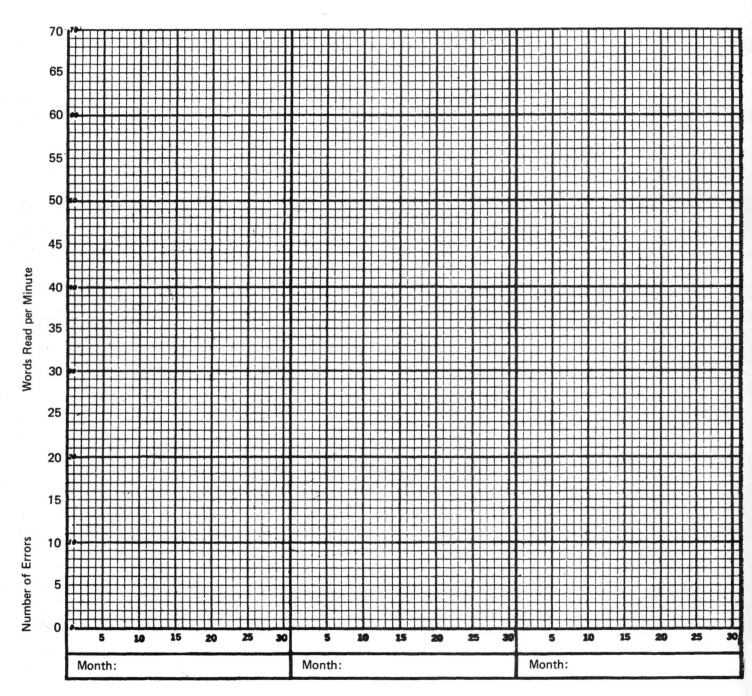

Calendar Days

72

PROFICIENCY GRAPH

Student_____

Goal_____

●———————● Words Read Correctly

✕———————✕ Errors

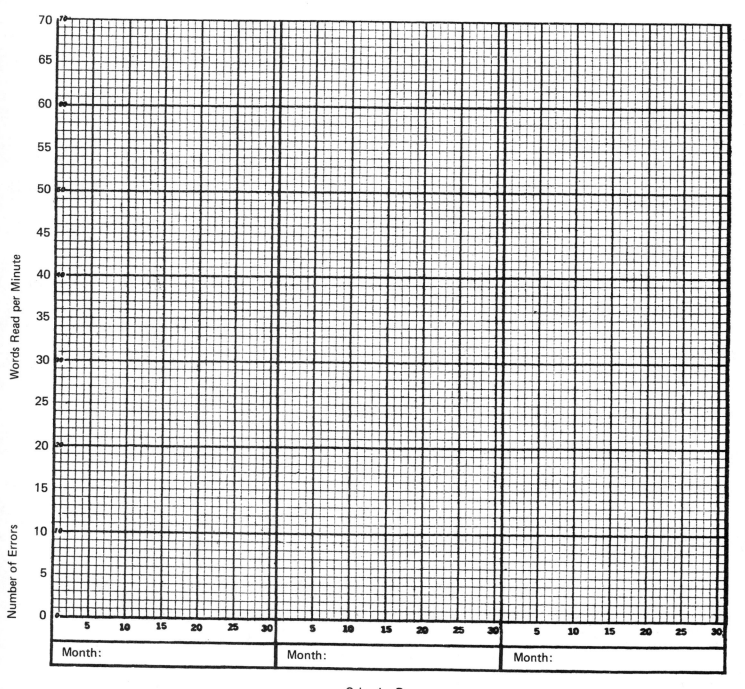

Words Read per Minute

Number of Errors

Month: Month: Month:

Calendar Days

73

Dictation

EXAMINER'S RECORDING FORM—READING

Check Test: Lists 15-19

Megawords 3

Name _____   Date _____

15. /əl/ and /ĭk/ Endings

reversal
frantic
electric
interval
loyal

correct _____

16. /ĭt/ and /ət/ Endings

delicate
velvet
favorite
deposit
moderate

correct _____

17. Middle-Syllable Schwa

execute
buffalo
balcony
singular
emphasize

correct _____

18. /ənt/ and /əns/ Endings

ignorant
resistance
resident
presence
attendance

correct _____

19. Unaccented Endings

masculine
practice
detective
certain
magazine

correct _____

Total Correct _____
Total Possible __25__

Name_____ Date_____

15. /əl/ and /ĭk/ Endings

reversal
frantic
electric
interval
loyal

correct_____

16. /ĭt/ and /ət/ Endings

delicate
velvet
favorite
deposit
moderate

correct_____

17. Middle-Syllable Schwa

execute
buffalo
balcony
singular
emphasize

correct_____

18. /ənt/ and /əns/ Endings

ignorant
resistance
resident
presence
attendance

correct_____

19. Unaccented Endings

masculine
practice
detective
certain
magazine

correct_____

Total Correct_____
Total Possible__25__

76